Charities at work

Protecting the
ENVIRONMENT

Diane Church

W
FRANKLIN WATTS
LONDON•SYDNEY

First published in Great Britain by
Franklin Watts
96 Leonard Street
London EC2A 4XD

Franklin Watts Australia
56 O'Riordan Street
Alexandria
NSW 2015

ISBN: 0 7496 4075 8
Dewey Decimal Classification 304.2
A CIP catalogue record for this book is available from the British Library

Printed in Malaysia

Editor: Kate Banham
Designer: Kirstie Billingham
Art Direction: Peter Scoulding

Acknowledgements
The publishers would like to thank the following organisations
for their permission to reproduce photographs in this book:
BTCV: front cover (Rob Bowker); Centre for Alternative Technololgy: p. 18l; DigitalVision: pp. 14, 18r;
Farming and Wildlife Advisory Group: p. 13 (J. Nourish); Franklin Watts Photo Library: pp. 4, 7b (Chris Fairclough),
16t (Chris Fairclough), 17b (Chris Fairclough), 19t (Chris Fairclough), 19b; Friends of the Earth: pp. 6, 7t;
Greenpeace: pp. 5b, 9t, 9b, 10 (© Greenpeace/Grace), 24; Land Heritage: p. 12; Landmark Trust: p. 21;
Marine Conservation Society: p. 11b (F. Tyson); National Trust Photo Library: pp. 20t (Joe Cornish), 20b (Ian Shaw);
Rainforest Concern: pp. 5t, 8 (Michael Dilger); Sustrans: pp. 15 both (Julia Bayne), 25 (Julia Bayne); Waste Watch: p. 17t;
WWF-UK: pp 11t (Richard Hartnell), 22 (Philip Nixon), 23 both (Mark Edwards)

Contents

Words printed in **bold** are explained in the glossary.

♥ The world around us

The **environment** is the place where you live: your bedroom, your house, your town, your district, your country and your world.

Looking after your room and keeping it tidy is not very exciting, but it's easy. Caring for the world around us is much more difficult. Many places have been very badly damaged.

This is because there are more people in the world than there used to be. It is also because we produce, use and throw away many more things than in the past.

The things we use make lots of litter that is very wasteful.

This book explains how charities are trying to stop this damage and what we can all do to help.

In the last 30 years, people have destroyed more than 30 percent of the world's forests.

We can help protect the environment by carefully choosing what food we eat. Charities explain which foodstuffs are best.

What happens to your rubbish when you throw it in the bin?

Protecting natural areas - locally

Have you ever visited any unspoilt areas? They have taken hundreds of years to form and are home to an amazing range of plants and **wildlife**. But they are gradually being destroyed or damaged by people.

CASE STUDY

Friends of the Earth is trying to make sure that no more peat is taken from Hatfield, one of the UK's last areas of bog land. Peat is a very rich soil and, if it is removed, many rare insects will die and the animals that feed on them will disappear too.

Peat is used by gardeners to make their plants grow stronger, although home-made compost works well too.

The Council for the Protection of Rural England (CPRE) stops lots of new houses being built on unspoilt land. The CPRE wants more old buildings in towns and cities to be turned into housing.

Have any new homes been built in your area? What was on the land before?

♥ Protecting natural areas - worldwide

Around the world many natural areas are being destroyed or adapted to provide us all with the things we want. Some of the oldest forests in Vietnam have been chopped down for wood to make garden furniture. Rainforests have been destroyed so that cattle can be farmed for hamburgers.

CASE STUDY

At Rainforest Concern you can buy a piece of rainforest in South America to help protect rare animals and plants. If the rainforests are destroyed, thousands of types of animals and plants, like these orchids, may disappear forever.

Greenpeace worked with other charities to protect 20 valleys in Canada's Great Bear Rainforest. The area is home to wolves, bears and other beautiful animals.

Look at some of the things you own. Where were they made?

The trees in this forest are huge. If they are cut down, they take hundreds of years to grow again.

♥ Saving the seas

Do you like fish and chips? If you do, you should know that cod – one of the most popular fishes we eat – is disappearing from our seas. This is because cod, like many other fish, are being caught before they have grown up and had a chance to breed.

Many sea creatures are killed by fishing with driftnets. These are nets that hang in the sea and catch everything that swims into them.

This diver is freeing a sunfish from a driftnet.

WWF – the global environmental network – has a yellow submarine. It has travelled around the country to help make people realise the damage being done to the seas and how they can help.

Every day, five million items of waste are thrown into the sea. The Marine **Conservation** Society has a Beachwatch scheme. Local people save animals and protect plants by clearing up the rubbish that gets washed on to the beaches.

Make sure you take your rubbish home when you visit the seaside.

♥ The changing countryside

You may think that the countryside hasn't changed much for many years. But it has. Fields are bigger, hedges have been removed and more chemicals are used to produce larger amounts of food. All this has damaged the environment.

⬆ These children are learning how to look after flowers and plants in the countryside.

Land Heritage owns farmland that grows **organic** food. This means it is grown without using chemicals. The charity also owns a children's farm that shows children how to make compost, grow seeds and find out about small animals like newts and frogs.

Since 1945, 97 percent of flower-rich meadows and 304,000 km of woodland have been lost to farmland or building. These areas were once home to birds and small animals.

What changes have you noticed or heard about in the countryside?

♥ Transport

How do you get to school or go to the shops? More and more journeys - even short trips that could be easily walked or cycled - are being made in the car.

Car exhaust fumes make the air bad for breathing.

Traffic fumes contain some of the most dangerous chemicals known to man. These fumes are one reason why the **ozone layer** - which protects us from the harmful rays of the Sun - has been damaged.

The charity Sustrans has set up a scheme called Safe Routes to School to get more children walking and cycling to school. It aims to reduce traffic and help children get fitter.

CASE STUDY

At St Mary's Primary School in Bristol, many more children now cycle since Sustrans helped work out six safe routes to the school. 'My mum used to bring me to school in the car,' says eight-year-old Callum. 'Now I ride my bike, meet up with my friends on the way and am wide awake when I get to class.'

Do you sometimes go by car when you could walk or cycle? How can people be encouraged to use their cars less?

♡ Waste and recycling

What happens to your rubbish when you throw it in the bin? Empty drinks cans, **disposable** nappies, old clothes, broken electrical goods – all have to go somewhere. Most of the time, they are buried in the ground, dumped at sea or burnt. All of these ways cause problems for the environment.

Eight million disposable nappies are thrown away every day in the UK.

CASE STUDY

Gina set up the Real Nappy Association eight years ago when she had her first baby, Mark. She wanted to help parents get **reusable** fabric nappies that can be washed again and again. 'At the time it was impossible to find them anywhere. Disposable nappies still cause a huge amount of waste,' says Gina.

Waste Watch has a helpline and website that gives lots of suggestions to help reduce rubbish.

The Waste Watch website tells people what things can be recycled and where to take them.

Many towns have special bins where you can recycle paper, cans, bottles, clothes and even books.

What things, if any, do you **recycle**? Find out what else you could recycle.

♡ Saving energy

Switching on a light, listening to a CD, cooking a meal... everything you do uses energy. At the moment we are all using up some of the world's energy sources, like oil, gas and coal, much faster than they are produced. Burning fossil fuels such as coal causes **global warming**.

The Centre for Alternative Technology in Wales shows people how to use the Sun and water to make energy in ways that do not harm the environment.

The wind is a good source of energy and, unlike coal, oil or gas, it will never run out.

Much of the food we buy has been grown in distant countries. Aeroplanes use a lot of fuel to bring the food here. Energy is also used to make the packaging that protects the food on its journey.

Friends of the Earth has launched a campaign – Real Food – to get people to buy food that's better for the environment. That includes food grown locally which uses less energy to transport it to shops and markets.

Markets are good places to buy locally-grown fruit and vegetables.

Look at the labels on the food you eat. How far has it travelled to reach you?

♥ Land and buildings

How do you and your family look after your home? You probably do some cleaning and every few years you may have to decorate. If you have a garden, you may help care for the plants or cut the grass.

In the UK, there are lots of old buildings and open spaces that need to be cared for.

⬆ The National Trust protects and looks after beaches and large areas of countryside in the UK, so that we can enjoy them.

CASE STUDY

The Landmark Trust rescues interesting and historic old buildings that have become very run down, and restores them to how they would have looked when they were built. The buildings are then rented out for holidays. These two pictures show the Langley Gatehouse in Shropshire. The top picture shows how it used to look, and the bottom picture show how it looks since the Landmark Trust restored it.

♡ Think globally, act locally

Natural **habitats** are disappearing; some animals and plants are dying out; and the seas and land are becoming filled with rubbish.

To help save the world from further damage, we need to change the way we live. WWF works with schools to explore how young people, and their friends and families, can take better care of the environment.

CASE STUDY

Staff and pupils at Cassop Primary School, Durham, were presented with a gold award by WWF for their clever use of a wind turbine in the school grounds. This supplies all the electricity the school needs. They also save water, use paper on both sides and clear litter. They have set up a recycling scheme in their village, and they get people to make compost from their rubbish. They even grow and eat their own vegetables.

Some schools collect old newspapers and magazines for recycling. This helps to save trees from being cut down.

We are all using much more water than we used to: in baths, washing machines, dishwashers and on our gardens. This is draining the rivers dry which threatens wildlife.

These children have used the water they wash their hands with to help grow vegetables.

Charities are able to help others because they are given money. This money comes from **governments**, businesses and people like you and me. Together we raise millions of pounds for charity each year.

This man is dressed as a mountie (a Canadian mounted policeman) to raise money and attract people's attention to the Greenpeace campaign.

There are many fun ways to raise money for charity. It doesn't matter how silly or simple the idea is - as long as it helps.

A sponsored bike ride is a good way to raise money.

Can you think of something your class could do to get people thinking about the environment and raise money? How about a rubbish auction or a tidiest (or untidiest) room competition?

♥ Do your bit

One of the best ways of helping to protect the environment is by doing what you can to reduce, reuse and recycle things. You can also encourage your family and friends to do the same.

You can save energy by:
- switching off the lights, your computer, the television or radio when you are not using them
- getting your family to buy food from local shops and markets
- not taking carrier bags or packaging from shops unless necessary
- drying your clothes on a washing line rather than using a tumble drier

You can save water by:
- having a shower rather than a bath
- not leaving taps running
- washing your car or bike with a bucket, rather than a hose
- watering the garden with a watering can not a hose
- getting your parents to wash clothes on the shortest cycle on the washing machine. This saves energy too.

You can save paper by:
- drawing on the back of old paper
- cutting up used paper and making it into small pads to use as rough paper
- recycling old newspapers, magazines and cardboard
- sharing your comics with friends, and then giving them to the local hospital
- checking the 'print preview' on your computer before printing to avoid unnecessary mistakes

You can recycle and reuse things by:
- going to bottle, paper and aluminium can banks
- getting your family to use a compost bin or wormery (or better still, make your own!)
- buying things that can be used more than once

You can encourage wildlife by:
- putting up a bird table, or a bird or bat box
- not using unnecessary chemicals in the garden like weed killers and pest-control products

You can save fuel by:
- walking or cycling to school or by giving friends a lift in the car

You can protect the environment by:
- never picking wild flowers
- keeping to proper tracks in the countryside
- not disturbing wildlife in pools
- taking rubbish home

♥ How you can help

If you care about the environment, you can help by:

● contacting a charity that you are interested in (see pages 30-31) to find out more about what they do. Many charities have children's clubs that include competitions and games, as well as providing information.

● asking your teacher to get someone from an environmental charity to come and talk to your class.

● looking up (after getting permission from your parents or teacher) one of the environmental charity websites.

● following the advice in this book on how to reduce, reuse and recycle and by encouraging your family and friends to do the same.

● raising some money for the environmental charity of your choice on your own or through your school. Get your parent, carer or teacher to contact the charity to find out more.

Glossary

compost	a type of soil that can be made from garden waste and kitchen scraps
conservation	to save something from being destroyed
disposable	something you use once and throw away
environment	the world around us including plants, animals, buildings and the sea
government	the people who make laws and rule the country
global warming	burning fossil fuels like coal makes the world hotter. This is causing ice to melt, sea levels to rise and people living in low-lying countries are being flooded.
habitat	the natural environment of a plant or animal where it grows and lives.
organic	produced without using chemicals
ozone layer	a layer of gas high above the Earth's surface that protects us from the Sun's harmful rays
recycle	to take an object or material and use it to make something else
reuse	to use things again and again
wildlife	animals and plants that live in the wild

♥ Contact details

All of the charities in this book work hard to help the environment. Contact them to find out more.

Centre for Alternative Technology
01654 702400
www.cat.org.uk
ata@cat.org.uk

Council for the Protection of Rural England [CPRE]
020 7976 6433
www.cpre.org.uk

Farming and Wildlife Advisory Group
024 7669 6699
www.fwag.org.uk

Friends of the Earth - England, Wales and Northern Ireland
020 7490 1555
www.foe.co.uk
info@foe.co.uk

Greenpeace
020 7865 8100
www.greenpeace.org.uk

Land Heritage
01647 61099
www.landheritage.org

Landmark Trust
01628 825925
www.landmarktrust.co.uk

Marine Conservation Society
01989 566017
www.mcsuk.org

National Trust
020 7222 9251
www.nationaltrust.org.uk
enquiries@ntrust.org.uk

Rainforest Concern
020 7229 2093
www.rainforest.org.uk
rainforest@gn.apc.org

Real Nappy Association
020 8299 4519
www.realnappy.com

Sustrans
0117 929 0888
www.sustrans.org.uk
info@sustrans.org.uk

Waste Watch
020 7253 6266
Wasteline no: 08702 430136
www.wastewatch.org.uk

WWF-UK
01483 426444
www.wwf-uk.org
Teacher enquiries to:
sking@wwf.org.uk

Organisations in Australia and New Zealand

Australian Conservation Foundation Inc.
(03) 9416 1166
www.acfonline.org.au

Database of Australian Charities
www.auscharity.org.au

Greenpeace
09-6306317

Kids Earth Fund
(02) 9261 4084
www.kidsearthfund.org.au
info@kidsearthfund.org.au

♥ Index